TABLE C

PART III

PREFACE

"I never forget a face, but in your case I'll gladly make an exception."
– Groucho Marx

It was a sunny evening in Paris, France, and I was sitting in a bar with my new girlfriend (Let's call her "Emma"). We were waiting to meet, for the first time, her best friend—a guy named Jack. After a while, a guy came over, hugged Emma, shook my hand and was introduced as "Nicolas." Turns out he was just another male friend who happened to be at the bar at the same time. Emma and Nicolas chatted for a bit, and then finally Jack turned up.

Bear in mind the fact that I had only been seeing Emma for about six weeks when I tell you that it was then slightly disarming to see her chatting away, laughing at these guys jokes (especially Jack's) and generally making me feel like I wasn't in the room. The situation wasn't helped by the fact that their English wasn't exactly fluent, and so while they chatted up a storm with Emma in French, I was left smiling along as best as could.

I left to get another drink and, while waiting at the bar, saw three other guys join Emma's table. Okay, so I knew other friends might be joining us later, but I didn't know they were all dudes. Now, I wasn't someone who usually begrudged girlfriends' their male friends, but the sight of Emma sitting there surrounded by five guys left me feeling decidedly uneasy. Clutching my drink, I made my way back to the group and tried to pretend I wasn't having a mini-nervous breakdown.

Over the coming months, a few facts about Emma's relationship with her best friend, Jack, became apparent. Firstly it became apparent that they messaged each other on Facebook practically every day. Then, it turned out that they had met in a club seven years ago and kissed on a first date. As much as Emma tried to reassure me that this kiss confirmed there was "zero sexual chemistry" between them, the die was cast...

And, that ladies and gentlemen, was the start of my descent into relationship jealousy hell. A nagging unease, underlying anger and growing jealousy began to grow and grow the more I thought about Emma's male friends and, in particular, a certain Jack. The more questions I asked about their relationship, the more angry and jealous I got. And the more angry and jealous I got, the more I ended up pushing Emma away—giving her the third degree over *any* conversation she had with a man, quizzing her on where she was going and who she was meeting, invading her personal privacy and generally acting like a crazy person. I tried *everything* to stop feeling how I was feeling—from trawling the internet for information, to talking to Emma about it, to writing each other love letters, but nothing seemed to work.

As you've purchased this book, chances are that you're also racked by a similar form of useless jealous monkey chatter going on in your brain about your partner's imaginary infidelity that I went through. Maybe you've asked for help with your jealousy and been told, "Just learn to trust them and everything will be alright," "Stop, or you'll ruin the relationship,""Get over it," and so on. As well-intentioned as these nuggets of wisdom are, they're of little use to the sufferer of relationship jealousy. Intellectually you know you they're right—you should just "get over it"—*but how?* Well, don't worry, this book will show you how.

In all the time I was plagued by jealousy and searching for the answer, *something was working...* My mind was taking on board a substantial amount of information as I searched for the answer, often by looking deep within myself. As time went on I began to realize that certain positive thoughts, concepts, and actions seriously helped to quell jealous feelings more than others, and herein lies the genesis of this book. I ended up focusing on several key concepts that really helped me to see my situation in a much clearer light. Within a couple of weeks these concepts—coupled with the daily practical exercises in steps nine to twelve—had eliminated my jealous thoughts.

Some time afterwards, I decided to write this book to help fellow sufferers of this debilitating and confusing condition regain control of their mind and their relationship.

Although I can say with confidence that my jealousy has now disappeared, let me stress that I have absolutely no qualifications or special skills to back up this book other than my direct experience. I am not a psychologist or a doctor. I'm just a regular guy who has successfully squashed a set of irrational thoughts and behaviors after a long and protracted struggle, and ultimately by myself. —

I wrote this book for you, because I want you to be able to shake off the curse of jealousy much quicker than I did, and finally be able to stop spending emotional energy on problems that don't even exist.

Note: I'll be referring throughout the book to a "Resources Toolkit" which contains videos, books and blog posts you can check out for further information on whatever subject I'm talking about.

You can find it online at:

www.retroactivejealousycrusher.com/resourcestoolkit/

INTRO

Imagine for a moment two ducks swimming in a lake. Everything's calm and peaceful. Then, one duck decides to attack the other duck. There's a flapping of wings, splashing of water and maybe some squawking, but just as suddenly as the conflict began, it's over. The two ducks swim away from each other like nothing happened.

In this regard, people should be more like ducks. We should be able to brush off altercations, thoughts, emotions and just get on with our day without them ever bothering us again. But the majority of us find this extremely difficult. Whether it's remaining angry about an argument for days, or ruminating on a grudge, or obsessing over our past, we humans love hanging on to things that we should probably just let go. This is the aim of this book: to enable you to let go of the constant stream of anxious thoughts, emotions and behaviors you currently have surrounding your partner's relationships with other people of the opposite sex (or same sex, depending on your preferences).

So, how do we do this? We do it in three parts…

PART I: UNDERSTANDING RELATIONSHIP JEALOUSY

I believe it's essential to understand fully what you're up against before you can tackle it, and the first four steps in the book address this head on. A major part of the problem with jealousy in a relationship is confusion over what exactly it is you are tackling. Are these negative emotions and thoughts a product of anger? Fear? Not feeling special to your partner? Being judgmental? Or all of the above?

The mind feeds off the puzzle, and the confusing nature of what exactly it is that you're feeling makes it that much harder to combat. It's like trying to play pool while drunk, wearing a blindfold and holding the cue round the wrong way. Not that I've ever tried that, but you get the picture.

In these steps, however, I detail the exact nature of jealousy in a relationship and the two key emotions driving it, so you'll know exactly what it is you're feeling and be better equipped to fight it.

PART II: REWIRING YOUR MIND

Once you know what relationship jealousy is and what's causing it, I'll show you how to rewire the mind so you no longer have it. This section focuses on negating the *two key emotions* that are causing your jealousy. You will learn how to rewire the mind to rid it of the negative, limiting beliefs it currently has, and replace them with four new beliefs which will change how you think about yourself and your partner.

When these four new concepts have been taken on board, you will have the solid foundation necessary to tackle the practical exercises outlined in the final section.

PART III: LET'S GET PRACTICAL

Changing the way you think about certain concepts is an essential step on the road to overcoming the affliction, but the mind will attempt to resist this at all costs, unless it is backed up by action. And that's where this final section comes in, as it's only through action rather than mere thoughts that we can truly "rewire" the mind to do what we want it to do. So, in Part III, I detail four helpful, practical exercises you can do every day in order to kill your jealousy for good.

A short note: this book is written from the perspective of a heterosexual male, but the scourge of jealousy in a relationship can strike at any gender or sexuality. Whether you are gay, straight, black, white, male, female, vegetable or mineral, this book will help ease your suffering and hopefully banish it for good.

Also, I suggest you buy yourself a new notepad. We'll be doing exercises during the book that require writing things down, and it's good to use a fresh pad exclusively for relationship jealousy.

So, once you're ready, let's begin…

PART I

UNDERSTANDING
RELATIONSHIP JEALOUSY

STEP ONE

WAY BACK IN THE DAY

"Evolution has meant that our prefrontal lobes are too small, our adrenal glands are too big, and our reproductive organs apparently designed by committee; a recipe which, alone or in combination, is very certain to lead to some unhappiness and disorder."
– Christopher Hitchens

If we trace the evolutionary history of humankind, we find that part of the reason we suffer from jealous thoughts and emotions about our partners, is because it has been hardwired into us since the dawn of time to do so. Without delving too much into evolutionary science, both men and women seem to be programed to be naturally wary of the opposite sex when it comes to our partners and the risk of them being unfaithful. As a broad generalization, men tend to be more worried more about sexual infidelity, and women about emotional infidelity.

SEXUAL INFIDELITY

For men, this evolutionary programing is the reason why they often don't really care as much about being "emotionally" cheated on as they do about being "physically" cheated on. In other words, if a man's wife confesses to having developed feelings for a guy at work, but nothing physical has happened between them, this is probably less devastating than if she confessed to spending one night of passion with him.

This is because, generally speaking, men have evolved to be super-wary their partner's sexual activity and relationships with other males. Multiple, casual, sexual encounters and/or the ability to easily form friendships with other men symbolically represent a higher risk of a woman being promiscuous and therefore potentially unfaithful. In evolutionary terms this raises the fear that he could end up raising a child which is not his own, and herein lies one of the major root causes of relationship jealousy in men.

EMOTIONAL INFIDELITY

Women, on the other hand, tend to be more worried about emotional infidelity because, back in the dawn of time, they had to place more emphasis on making sure a man stuck around to help them raise their child. Consequently women are now far more likely, in terms of relationship jealousy, to have anxiety over who their man might end up dating or fall in love with. This is because if he ends up possibly harboring feelings for someone else, he may leave to be with that other woman, leaving her to raise a child alone.

It is quite an important step to realize that these negative thoughts and emotions you're experiencing are in reality merely a product of your evolutionary history and, therefore, not necessarily "your fault." So don't be so hard on yourself! In order to bring this theory a little bit more up to date, let's take a quick look at how evolution has shaped our minds to behave this way—the thing that is the single biggest cause of human suffering since the beginning of time…

THE EGO

The ego is not just an "inflated sense of self." It's *your mind's perception of self*, whether it happens to be inflated or not. By "perception of self" I mean anything that you identify strongly with and regard as "you." This could be anything from your name, to your favorite band, or variety of frozen yoghurt. Anything with which you form a strong mental attachment becomes part of your sense of self and therefore you ego—or, the part of your mind which says, "this is me." So, whenever you, or someone else says, "I hate musicals," or, "I love wrestling," or, "I'm a member of X political party and I support everything they say!" that's the ego talking. However, when the mind identifies a little too strongly with the ego and listens to it too much, it can cause problems.

Every bad emotion, argument, fight and war can trace its origins back to the ego. This is because it represents a very black and white view of the world which, in trying to protect us and the things we value, actually does nothing but hold us back and cause pain and suffering.

Our partners, of course, get wrapped up by our ego's into this rigid sense of self. So, when it perceives a threat to our partner, i.e. from an outside attack of another man or woman, it jumps into action to protect itself (us). Much like how, thousands of years ago, our egoic mind made us run when confronted with an on-rushing bear, today it is operating in the exact same mode of self-preservation when confronted with the perceived threat of your partner having sex with or falling in love with someone else. By keeping you in a constant state of anxiety regarding your partner's behavior, it's trying to protect you from harm, (i.e. being cheated on) by making you think, *"What are his real intentions?" "Is she a threat?" "Do I really want to be with someone who likes [insert 'best friend of the opposite sex']?"*

Your ego is in the driving seat when you are gripped by jealousy in a relationship. Now, this may all sound a little "new agey" if you're not familiar with it, but it's important to remember that your ego isn't "you" or your true self. Your ego is an illusion. Your true self is "consciousness," "awareness," or whatever you wish to call it, and embraces the present moment, while your ego fears it. In other words, *you* are not really jealous, upset or anxious about your partner's behavior, or threatened by their attractive friends. Your ego is merely tricking you into *believing* you are. In a way, however, it's a good thing that your ego has created this jealousy in your relationship. It means your mind is functioning normally and is just trying to protect you, as it should. The problem of course arises when the ego takes over, balloons the threat out of all proportion and traps the mind in its own prison of repetitive, unwanted thoughts, emotions and behaviors.

Before we tackle the ego full on in later steps, here's a little exercise you can start right now to help you learn more about how it operates. Take a moment to "watch" your ego. Start by having a think about something that bothers or annoys you.

Your relationship jealousy would be the obvious thing, but focus on something else for now—something like a situation at work, or an argument. Dwell on these thoughts and feelings. Think about all ways you've been "wronged," or what you should've said but didn't. Now have a go at noticing them, rather than reacting to them. Step back and observe these thoughts and emotions whirling away inside you. Become aware that this negativity, which positions you as "the victim," fighting against an imaginary "enemy," is coming from your ego.

HOW TO "WATCH" YOUR EGO

Before we tackle the ego full on in later steps, take a moment to "watch" your ego. Start by having a think about something that bothers or annoys you. Retroactive jealousy would be the obvious thing, but focus on something else for now—something like a situation at work, or an argument. Dwell on these thoughts and feelings. Think about all ways you've been "wronged," or what you should've said but didn't. Now have a go at noticing them, rather than reacting to them. Step back and observe these thoughts and emotions whirling away inside you. Become aware that this negativity, which positions you as "the victim," fighting against an imaginary "enemy," is coming from your ego.

I will go into this in more depth later. For now, just practice noticing whenever you become lost in negative thoughts and emotions during the day, and try to realize each time that this is your ego talking, and not necessarily "you." In the Resources Toolkit you'll find more information on the ego from philosopher, Sam Harris, and Eckhart Tolle, among others.

STEP TWO

THOUGHTS & EMOTIONS

"We are dying from overthinking. We are slowly killing ourselves by thinking about everything. Think. Think. Think. You can never trust the human mind anyway. It's a death trap."
– Anthony Hopkins

So, you've realized that your partner gets hit on when they go out, or that they find their friend good-looking, and now you can't get the nagging sensation that they're one step away from leaving you out of your head. A vicious circle of unwanted thoughts and emotions has, unfortunately, been triggered within you. This leads to jealous actions, such as questioning, snooping and accusing. Let's take a look at each of these phenomena—emotions, thoughts and actions—in turn to see exactly what's going on with each of them.

EMOTIONS

Negative emotions about your partner's behavior and whether or not they can be trusted are the ground zero of relationship jealousy. If you reflected on their choices involving people of the opposite sex positively, you would not have negative emotions and consequently wouldn't suffer from anxious thoughts and behaviors.

Sean Webb, founder of the groundbreaking website *I Am Spirituality,* has developed an easily understood equation which explains how emotions work within each and every one of us. It goes like this:

$$(EP - RP = ER)$$

Expectation or Preference – Reality as Perceived = Emotional Response

Okay, so what does this mean? In a nutshell, our Expectation or Preference is how we would like, or expect, something we're emotionally attached to, to be or turn out. Our Reality as Perceived is then how something actually is, or what actually happens. And finally, our Emotional Response is conditioned by this Reality as Perceived. In other words, if our Reality as Perceived meets our Expectation or Preference, we experience a positive emotion. If it falls below our Expectation or Preference, we experience a negative emotion.

Sean Webb tackles many emotions on his site, but doesn't really go into jealousy of any kind, and so here's a brief analysis of how your emotions are working when applied to jealousy in a relationship. Your Emotional Preference is that, for example, your boyfriend only has male friends, never talks to women when he goes out, and has only ever enjoyed sex within a secure monogamous relationship. The Reality as Perceived is when you realize one of his best friends is a girl he thinks is good looking, he enjoys chatting to women when he goes out and has had a "promiscuous" past. Therefore, you experience a negative Emotional Response. But, in order for you to have an Emotional Response of any kind, you must have an emotional attachment to the thing you're reacting to.

In the case of jealousy in a relationship, the reason why you have such a strong emotional reaction, is because you have formed a strong emotional attachment to your partner. The more you care for someone, the more susceptible you are to being attacked by relationship jealousy. One of my exes had a male best friend who she'd slept with a couple of times in the past, and yet I didn't care. Okay, so I didn't *like* the fact that he'd had sex with my girlfriend particularly, but it wasn't something I obsessed over. I just forgot about it. But, even though Emma's relationship with Jack is somewhat less colorful than this particular ex's, I became consumed by jealous thoughts about it because my emotional attachment to her is that much greater.

THOUGHTS

As I've already stated, it is these negative emotions which are causing you to suffer from negative thoughts about your partner's trustworthiness and relationships with the opposite sex. Thoughts which are particularly pernicious because they make you act in ways you normally wouldn't.

Trying to stop thinking about "that guy who's always messaging her on What's App," or "that girl he talked to at the bar," only makes you think about these things even more, as your mind descends into a "don't think about a pink elephant"-type war with itself. The thoughts are then subsequently given even more power, making the emotions even more negative toward your partner (and yourself.) As the influential author, Eckhart Tolle, has observed—your thoughts seem to be controlling you rather than the other way around.

The funny thing is, these thoughts are almost certainly not even accurate. They're just manifestations within a mind that knows nothing of what's really happening, but wants to assume the worst. How do you *know* that your girlfriend is mentally undressing every man she talks to? Or that your boyfriend is friends with Mandy at work because he wants to start an affair? The mind paints a picture of these worst case scenarios because it wants you to see things in a negative rather than positive light in an effort to protect you, but the reality is probably very different.

ACTIONS

This concoction of negative emotions and repetitive thoughts, feeds in to jealousy driven actions. These actions are, in part, a manifestation of your need for control over your partner's actions in order to reassure yourself that they won't hurt you. The obvious examples are the wife who demands her husband text him every half hour they're apart. Or the boyfriend who can't stand the thought of his girlfriend going out on the town and spies on her leaving a club at 3 a.m. Even if you're not as extreme as the people in these examples, you probably, on some level at least, feel the need to control your partner.

Consciously or subconsciously, you want to control your partner because you fear they may leave you, and so are wary of any kind of emotional or sexual connection between them and other people. By checking up on them all the time, you think you're somehow making sure they don't cheat on you, when in actual fact you're more likely to bring about a self-fulfilling prophecy that causes them to grow dissatisfied and possibly leave you, which is the last thing you want.

It's important to stress just how toxic this kind of controlling behavior is to a relationship. Nobody likes to be told what to do and be made to account for themselves all the time. Ultimately, it's a very destructive way to behave and definitely not a healthy ingredient to have floating around in your relationship, but we'll tackle how to overcome this need for control in more detail later.

STEP THREE

KNOW YOUR ENEMY

"Named must your fear be, before banish it you can."
– Yoda

The reason why the emotions surrounding your jealousy can be so hard to pin down is because there's probably a whole mix of different ones going on at the same time. Depending on the person, there could be as many as five or six different emotions contributing to their jealousy. I believe, however, that the primary emotion driving relationship jealousy—present in every sufferer of the condition—is plain, good old fashioned, fear. Put simply, on some level you're scared of losing your partner, and this is how your mind/ego is choosing to deal with it. If you take only one thing away from reading this book, make it this: relationship jealousy is just a *manifestation in your mind of your own worst fears regarding the relationship.*

So, if you're a man, what's the worst possible thing you can imagine your girlfriend or wife doing to you?—yep, having sex with someone else. If you're female, the worst thing you can maybe imagine is your guy falling in love with someone else. But bear in mind that, very often, both sexes are afraid of both outcomes. It's very important to understand that these repetitive thoughts and emotions—going over and over in your mind like a broken record—are, in fact, representations of this worst fear, rather than literal ones.

Intellectually, you probably know that your partner has no real interest in running off with someone from their book club, but the reason why it appears to be a real possible outcome is because this other person is who your mind has latched onto as a representation of its own worst fear.

The other part of this fear is wrapped up in how you think your partner *feels* about other people. In some way you fear that if your partner holds a warm and fuzzy spot in their heart for a friend, a colleague at work, or even a random person who tries to chat them up in a bar, then this means they're not completely 100 percent yours in some way. And if they're not 100 percent yours, that means maybe there's a chance you are somehow not living up to their expectations and so they could find that missing percentage somewhere else.

The confusing nature of relationship jealousy is that, in your conscious mind (that is, your true, aware self), you might not actually think your partner will definitely sleep with, or fall in love with someone else, but in your subconscious mind (your ego), you probably have a general fear that they will grow dissatisfied with you and so, potentially, it could happen. Relationship jealousy is at its root a manifestation of this fear, and the repeated images and thoughts are simply your worst fears being played over and over again in your head.

THE AMYGDALA

When we get anxious and stressed about things like jealousy in a relationship, you may be surprised to learn that a part of our brains literally becomes "enflamed." The part that becomes enflamed is an almond shaped set of neurons located in the temporal lobe of the brain, known as the amygdala. This is where the emotion of fear is located, and where defense responses are mobilized when it thinks we're in danger. The on-rushing bear, the advancing man with a knife, the car out of control and, in this case, people who possibly pose a threat to your relationship.

When we become flooded with negative and stressful thoughts, the amygdala releases a whole host of chemicals such as adrenaline and cortisol which increase heart rate, blood pressure and literally damage the brain without us even realizing it. Just by thinking certain thoughts, choosing to perceive them the way you do, and by dwelling on them constantly, your brain and body are suffering by having to repeatedly activate their stress mechanisms. In fact, what you need to be doing is the complete opposite, i.e. replacing these stress responses with relaxation responses, which I will show you how to do in Step Ten.

STEP FOUR

AND KNOW YOURSELF

"Don't look at me in that tone of voice."
– Dorothy Parker

Now on to the second key emotion which is fueling your relationship jealousy—judgement. A big part of the reason why you're suffering from the condition is because, consciously or subconsciously, you're looking down on the choices your partner makes and the activities they indulge in, now and maybe in the past too. Judgment is often tied up in higher than average expectations. Whether through your upbringing, or experiences in life, you've maybe somehow learnt to expect your partners to live up to a set of lofty ideals when it comes to what relationships, love and commitment should mean.

These high moral values regarding love and sex, can often mean you end up viewing a partner as "flirty," their past as "slutty," and their behavior in a relationship as "questionable."

For example, I once viewed Emma as promiscuous, which was being judgmental about her former sex life. I also spent a great deal of time wringing my hands over the fact she communicated with Jack nearly every day on Facebook (how much is there to say to one person?), which was me being judgmental about her behavior.

The problem is that, by being judgmental, you can end up not only questioning your partner's choices, but also *them* as a person. You may even go so far as to wonder whether you're really compatible with them in the first place. Judgment can play havoc with the day-to-day life of your relationship. You may find yourself looking at your partner—completely innocently, say, picking out vegetables in a supermarket—and feeling judgmental, bitter, and angry toward them for no reason at all. It may not even matter, for example, whether they even particularly want to go out partying with their friends that night. The fact is, they're doing it! And you don't like it.

Suffice it to say, looking at your partner in this way is not a nice emotion to have and can be pretty toxic to a relationship. There are, of course, other factors mixed in the melting pot of why we suffer from relationship jealousy, but a very large chunk of them are of our own making when we take the moral high ground and decide to deem our partner's actions as somehow "not right." Personally, when I stopped being judgmental of Emma's behavior, my relationship jealousy took a *huge* step toward lifting, and I will show you how to do this in later steps.

WHY ARE YOU FEARFUL & JUDGMENTAL?

Before we go any further, let's try and pin down what exactly you're feeling and why. So grab your notebook and pen and let's get to it. Close your eyes and and take five minutes to dwell in a state of jealousy. Really try to resurrect these feelings, thoughts and emotions and just experience your jealousy for a minute or so. Why are you feeling jealous? Is it the thought of your partner falling in love with someone at work? Or having a one-night stand with someone they met in a bar? Or both? Now I want you to write down what you're feeling. What are these emotions exactly? Pure jealousy? Or are you also feeling angry? Anxious? Betrayed? Sad? Or all of the above? Just try to get down on paper as much as you can about how you feel in a free-flowing stream of consciousness.

Next, I want you to have a think about how your partner's behavior might be causing this emotional reaction. Put down on paper what your partner has done, or is doing, to make you feel jealous. Have they cheated on you in the past? Did they cheat on someone else before they met you? Are they flirtatious with other people? You've probably thought about these things already, but putting them down on paper will really help solidify in your mind just what you have to be worried about, and very often the realization that it's not that much is a good wake up call.

Finally, I want you to put down what may have happened in your past to cause you to be jealous now in the present. Did one of your parents have an affair and leave the family? Do you have a pervasive feeling of emptiness, or lack of self-worth? Were your parents critical or repressive when you were growing up? Or were you spoilt as a child? How we are raised as children has a huge influence over how we behave as adults and so, especially if your partner is doing nothing to provoke your jealousy, it's well worth having a general think about how your own upbringing may be doing it instead. By writing your thoughts and emotions down in this manner, you might be able to get a greater grasp on what exactly they are, which will help while reading the rest of this book.

PART II

REWIRING YOUR MIND

STEP FIVE

IT'S NOT YOU, IT'S ME

"Nothing, she already has Zlatan."
– Zlatan Ibrahimovic when asked what he's getting his wife for her birthday.

As we learned earlier, one of the main emotions fueling your jealousy is fear. On some level, you worry your partner will sleep with, or fall in love with, someone else. But how do we loosen the grip of the ego and rewire the mind to stop it being so fearful?

Firstly, let's take a look at just why you have this fear in the first place. After all, many other people have partners who flirt with other people, or have a best friend of the opposite sex, and yet don't fall victim to relationship jealousy. The reason they don't is probably because they have confidence in themselves and in the relationship. Relationship jealousy and a certain lack of self-confidence, however, go hand in hand.

Sufferers of the condition tend to be consumed by comparing themselves to other people in their partner's lives and coming off second best. In turn, this causes their interpretation of their partner's behavior to become all screwy, if you'll pardon the pun. If you perceive there may be "better" lovers than you out there, you're more likely to worry that your partner may leave you for someone else. Have a think about if, on some level, you feel insecure within yourself. Do you feel that you're somehow inadequate, and/or "not worthy" of your partner's love?

In order to rewire the mind to be less fearful, and release the grip of the ego, it is essential you take stock of your own self-confidence. You may feel (like I did) that you're pretty self confident and secure in the relationship, but maybe you should take a closer look... Deep down, there may be something that is making you feel insecure. You may think things are fine now, but somewhere inside, you probably fear this won't last. Ask yourself, if you were 100 percent super confident in yourself would you feel the way you do?

Do you think George Clooney cares at all about who his partner talks to when she goes out? Probably not. That's because with a fully confident state of mind it's virtually impossible to suffer from jealousy in a relationship. Remember the saying "You have to love yourself before you can love someone else?" Yes, it annoys me too. Like the phrase "Love will happen when you stop looking for it," it's pretty meaningless. However, battling relationship jealousy means starting to value yourself more, recognizing your strengths and weaknesses and accepting yourself for who you are—both the good and the bad.

Learn to love yourself instead of judge yourself. Learn to not be so hard on yourself for your own failings, or bad choices you made in the past. This changing of your perception of yourself from maybe a slightly negative one to a more positive one is one of the most important things you can do in your fight against jealousy. From "I don't really respect myself," to "I totally respect everything about myself." From "I don't know if I'm worthy of him," to "Of course I deserve to be with him." From "I hope she stays with me," to "I know she'll stay with me because I'm the best there is."

There's a ton of information out there on improving self-esteem that I don't have the space here to go into, however, the good news is that just by merely knowing that your fear is due to a lack of confidence/self love should immediately alleviate some of the pain. So, now that you know the problem, you can go about actively addressing it. This can be done by changing both your thoughts and your actions.

CHANGE YOUR THOUGHTS

Simply thinking certain thoughts repeatedly every day is a surprisingly effective way of making you actually believe them. By telling yourself every day that you're a confident person and truly deserve to be with your partner, your mind will begin to take on these attributes. I suggest writing down a personal statement about yourself and how wonderful you are, or a list of all your best qualities—all the things you're good at and all the reasons why your partner loves you. Really go to town describing how unique and special you are, and put down all your amazing qualities that are the reason why your partner wants to be with you and not some random person of the opposite sex. Imbibe these good vibrations about yourself, maybe through meditation (more on this later). Memorize them and repeat them to yourself as often as possible, but definitely first thing when you wake up and last thing before you go to bed. Change the way you think about yourself and pretty soon you'll discover the "threat" posed by these other people will dissolve into nothingness when compared to your greatness!

CHANGE YOUR ACTIONS

Is there something specific you can pinpoint as a cause of your insecurity? Write down all the ways you feel inadequate somehow. Write down what you don't respect about yourself. List all the things you judge about yourself, and the things you wish you were. Maybe you don't think you earn enough money? Or you think you're overweight? Or underweight? Have a good hard think about what it is about yourself that you're not so confident about—something that you fear your partner may find in someone else—and then get to work tackling it.

Anything you write down is what needs to be tackled head on, *through action*. Once you do, you'll find your relationship jealousy begin to feel more insignificant the more confident you become.

THE BIG TUNE UP

Part of the reason why you may be suffering from relationship jealousy could be that you're just not taking enough care of your health. As you know, what we eat and how much we exercise obviously has a major role to play in keeping our bodies healthy, but did you know just how big a role it plays in keeping our brains healthy too? An unhealthy lifestyle can not only harm your body and mind, but also your self-confidence, productivity and overall happiness. One of the best things you can do while navigating the choppy waters of relationship jealousy, is to give your body and mind a tune up. In this pdf, therefore, I'll be covering the three key areas of: diet, exercise and mental sharpness.

Don't worry, I'm not here to give you a lecture on how you need to turn into a teetotal, kale munching gym bunny. But if you think you could be healthier than you are at the moment, it's worth doing something about it, no matter how small. If you're already a health nut who's been on a paleo diet for a year and has 10 percent body fat, however, you can probably go ahead and skip this bonus. If not, let's kick off with some…

FOOD FOR THOUGHT

Let's face it, most of us know we should be eating healthier but struggle to ever put it into practice. Diets are began and promptly dropped after a few weeks when we fail to see any significant results, don't feel much better and can't stand the thought of another day eating something called "bone broth." Sticking to the latest crash diets like this, in which you're supposed to religiously count calories or cut out carbs, can be virtually impossible. Even the people who find some success and actually lose weight, often end up putting it back on and feeling even worse than they did beforehand.

Not to mention all the confusion that's out there on what you should and shouldn't be consuming. One minute turning vegan is the best thing you can possibly do, the next it causes cancer.

While diets that completely revolutionize your eating habits obviously work for some, I wasn't one of them. Instead, I found it easier to keep eating what I liked, but less of it. That meant smaller portions and sometimes skipping meals such as breakfast or lunch altogether. If you feel there's something you're going overboard with eating, now might be the time to tone it down.

Make a list of foodstuffs, such as meat, sweets, alcohol, etc. that you may be consuming too much of, and start consuming less. Or set yourself a challenge to give something up for a month, one at a time. The monthly schedule will not only give you a motivational goal to work toward, but also train your body to live without whatever it is you want to cut down on. After thirty days, you should find it easier to consume it more moderately. For example, after years of snacking on sweets and cakes throughout the day, I gave them up for a month and now only treat myself to something sweet on the weekend.

Breaking down the week like this is another way of making cutting down on certain foodstuffs easier, as it works on a hardship/reward framework. It's not so galling to turn down a donut on a Wednesday if you know you can have one on Saturday. If you want to give a structured diet a go, however, I suggest checking out some of the links in the Resources Toolkit, where I list several guys who can help you out. Overall, I would strongly recommend taking the steps now to improve your diet or else risk running into problems later in life that maybe could've been avoided. I'm not saying you have to turn into Gwyneth Paltrow, but start giving your body more of the right kind of fuel and it will thank you for it.

You may even start to see your jealous thoughts start to dissipate... What we eat obviously has a major part to play in how healthy our bodies are, but did you know just how big a role it plays in keeping our brains healthy too? While reading *The UltraMind Solution* by Mark Hyman, I was struck by the following section:

SEROTONIN: STAYING HAPPY

Do you have low serotonin levels? Take the following quiz to find out. In the box on the right, place a check for each positive answer. Then find out how severe your problem is by using the scoring key below.

SEROTONIN QUIZ

1. My head is full of ANTS (automatic negative thoughts).

2. I'm a glass half empty person.

3. I have low self esteem and self confidence.

4. I tend to have obsessive thoughts and behaviors.

5. I get the winter blues or have SAD (seasonal affective disorder).

6. I tend to be irritable, easily angered, and/or impatient.

7. I am shy and afraid of going out, or have a fear of heights, crowds, flying, and/or public speaking.

8. I feel anxious and have panic attacks.

9. I have trouble falling asleep.

10. I wake up in the middle of the night and have trouble getting back to sleep, or wake up too early.

11. I crave sweets or starchy carbs like bread and pasta.

12. I feel better when I exercise.

13. I have muscle aches, fibromyalgia, and/or jaw pain (TMJ).

14. I have been treated with and felt better when taking SSRIs (serotonin boosting antidepressants).

SCORING KEY

Score one point for each box you checked.

SCORE SEVERITY

0 – 4   You may have a slightly low level of serotonin.

5 – 7   You may have a moderately low level of serotonin.

8+   You may have a severely low level of serotonin.

If you scored highly on the test and are someone who doesn't take that much care of what they eat, this lifestyle is probably helping to fuel your jealousy without you even realizing it. So, especially if your crisis is particularly bad, maybe have a go at completing the six week program in the book. Mark Hyman explains exactly how to increase your serotonin and decrease your stress levels by introducing things like magnesium, vitamin B6, tryptophan and protein to your diet, while eliminating anything with high sugar content, allergies, infections and toxins.

LET'S GET PHYSICAL

If the thought of changing your diet was bad enough, how about the prospect of taking up regular exercise? If you didn't leap up and down at the prospect, shouting "Yes, let's do this!"

don't worry, I fully understand. A vast number of us haven't exercised in any meaningful way for years, so it's perfectly natural to feel a little nauseous at the thought of starting now. Engaging in a sport or joining a gym can be an expensive, boring and fairly obnoxious experience. And besides, where are you supposed to find the time?

However, it's been scientifically proven that people who do regular physical activity have:

Up to an 83% lower risk of arthritis
Up to a 68% lower risk of hip fracture
Up to a 50% lower risk of type 2 diabetes
Up to a 50% lower risk of colon cancer
Up to a 35% lower risk of coronary heart disease and stroke
Up to a 30% lower risk of depression
Up to a 30% lower risk of dementia
Up to a 30% lower risk of early death

Most importantly for sufferers of relationship jealousy, regular exercise also lowers stress levels, raises energy and mood levels and improves sleep patterns. In short, exercise has a major positive impact on the mind, much in the same way as diet.

By releasing serotonin and other soothing chemicals such as dopamine, regular physical activity kills stress, boosts and improves connections between nerve cells, releases tension and acts as a natural anti-depressant. But how do you suddenly start exercising again after fifteen years? Firstly, if you're not that way inclined, I'd avoid engaging in anything you don't actually enjoy on some level, like going to the gym or jogging round the block. You'll just get bored and frustrated and give up. So I'd recommend doing something you actually enjoy, such as maybe playing a sport with a friend.

Whatever form of exercise you choose, aim to increase your endurance levels and the performance of your heart through cardiovascular aerobic exercise. In general, you can consider yourself minimally fit if you can increase your heart rate to at least 100 beats per minute and keep it there for half an hour, for a period of twenty minutes daily or forty-five minutes three times a week. Ideally, aim to raise your heart rate to at least sixty percent of your maximum pulse rate—that is, the top speed your heart can beat and still pump blood around your body. Your maximum heart rate is 220 less your age. So if you're, say, twenty-five, you should aim for an exercise heart rate of 117 (220 - 25 = 195 x 0.6 = 117).

If you can't abide the thought of playing football, squash, or swimming, how about walking? In fact, this is probably one of the very best forms of exercise for the non-sporty as it enables you to get fit, measure your progress and listen to your favorite music or podcast at the same time. I'm not talking about ambling along, though. I'm talking about walking at a brisk pace—say a mile in under fifteen minutes—and increasing your speed the fitter you get. If you walk two miles in half an hour, five times a week, you'll be engaging in a healthy fitness regime that's totally free and easy.

Regarding those ailing muscles I mentioned earlier, aim to also lightly increase your body strength via muscle resistance exercises, such as push-ups, pull-ups and sit-ups and/or working with weights. But don't go overboard. Forget the mantra "no pain, no gain" for now or you'll probably put yourself in ER, especially if you haven't done much physical activity in a while. Start slowly and gradually begin to build up your workout regimen as your body acclimatizes to suddenly moving about more. And don't forget to remain flexible by stretching thoroughly before any form of physical activity, or by practicing yoga. The great thing is, you don't need to join a gym anymore to start this kind of training. It can be done using little more than a workout mat and a laptop in the comfort of your own home, and I include some great videos in the Resources Toolkit regarding this. But remember to check out the latest research findings and your doctor's recommendations before embarking on any form of repetitive exercise program.

I realize how hard it can be to commit to regular physical activity like this, but it will result in tremendous long term health benefits. After incorporating a regular exercise program into my week, for example, I soon felt much more energized. In the afternoon when normally I could be found lightly dozing face down on my keyboard, I felt much more "with it." And my self-confidence grew too.

THE MIND

According to the latest Nielsen Report on how much time each week we all spend watching TV, we're all doing far too much of it. Here's the weekly average time middle-aged Americans spend in front of the TV:

Age 35 to 49: 33 hours, 40 minutes
Age 50 to 64: 43 hours, 56 minutes

That's an awful lot of TV. A full time job, in fact. And that's not even counting all the gazing we do at other types of screens, such as computers and mobile devices. The British, apparently, spend more hours a day on their laptops and fiddling with their phones than they do asleep. Eight hours and forty-one minutes to be exact. While there's nothing intrinsically wrong with watching TV, or using phones and laptops, the key word here again is moderation.

I haven't got the space here to go into all the health problems associated with excessive use of these devices, but I will say that maybe this behavior is exacerbating your jealousy. In general, if you're spending more time during the day engaging with a screen than real life, then it's probably time to reassess your habits.

Here are three ways to get started today:

Cut down on the TV. If you're watching ten different shows each week, or tend to loll around on the couch just watching whatever comes on, maybe it's time to be a bit more ruthless when it comes to what get beams into your house. Personally I've never seen *Game of Thrones*, *Breaking Bad*, *The Wire* or whatever show is currently hot at the moment, so maybe I'm not the best qualified person to talk about this, but I'm pretty sure they're not all "required viewing." Give your viewing habits a review and see what can be ditched in order to get your total time spent watching TV down to twenty hours a week or lower.

Turn off your phone. I don't know what's happened to our society but it seems no one can get through ten minutes anymore without checking their cell phone: talking to friends/family, walking down the street, driving, going to sleep, waking up, watching a film *in a movie theater*... If this sounds like you, it's time to look up, put your shoulders back, take in your surroundings and start interacting with the world again. You're missing out on a million potential conversations when your head's buried in your phone. Again, try giving yourself "phone free" zones in which you turn it off and place it out of sight. An hour, a day, a week—anything that reconnects you to real life.

Step away from the computer. Sitting in a swivel chair staring at a computer screen is the default pose for many of us at work, but according to many studies the damaging effects on the body are as harmful as smoking. Sitting for just six hours a day leads to all kinds of scary problems such as loss of bone mass, bad posture, weight gain, higher cholesterol, heart disease and cancer. The good news, however, is that much of this can be mitigated by getting up and moving about every so often. Set an alarm to go off every hour or so and make sure you fully stretch your legs to get the circulation going again. A ten minute break per sitting hour is recommended but may not be practical, but aim to get up and move about as often as you can.

STEP SIX

YOUR MIND IS A LIAR

"I have spent most of my life worrying about things that have never happened."
– Mark Twain

Now, on to the other key emotion—judgement. This phenomena of judgment within jealousy took me ages to figure out exactly what was going on. I knew on some level that I was being judgmental, but at the same time I didn't *feel* like I was being judgmental. The sensation was just there, so to speak, without me being able to put my finger on it. As it turned out, the primary cause of my being judgmental was simply a lack of trust.

The reason why you might look down your nose in judgment at your partner's behavior, or expect them to meet your lofty ideals about love and commitment, is because deep down you still don't 100 percent trust them. In this step, though, I'm going to show you how to combat the emotion of judgment by rewiring the mind to trust your partner.

A TRUST TEST

Before we begin, it's a good idea to first ascertain just how much you trust your partner right now. Imagine for a moment that your partner is going on party holiday with their friends to a place full of people they find attractive. So, if they love beautiful blonde women, that could be Copenhagen. Or, say they love guys with an Irish accent, that could be Dublin. Imagine it's a Saturday night and you know they'll be out, quite possibly getting hit on by these people you know they find attractive. How does that make you feel?

1. "I don't care in the least. I just want him/her to have fun."
2. "It makes me feel uncomfortable, but I guess I'm okay."
3. "I can't stand it! I feel like jumping on a plane and surprising them in the bar!"

If you answered 1. then I'm not sure why you're reading this book, but chances are you answered 2. or, more likely, 3. And if so, keep reading.

JEALOUSY IS COMMON IN NEW RELATIONSHIPS

The early stages of relationships, when couples are getting to know one another, are the most fertile for jealousy to flourish. The condition is far more common in couples who have only been together for, let's say, three years or less, than those who have been together for longer than three years. Now, I'm not blaming my girlfriend for my past relationship jealousy, but I think her admittance that she sometimes flirted with other guys on nights out, and found Jack "good looking" definitely didn't help me to trust her during these early stages.

It does of course happen that some people suffer from relationship jealousy after fifteen years of marriage, but this is far less common. The reason is simply that the emotions of fear and insecurity found during the beginning stages of a relationship, are generally replaced by deeper levels of security and trust the longer you stay with someone. In order to expedite the process, though, it's important to understand that a lack of trust may well be the reason why you're feeling judgmental, and that it's something you need to work on.

GAG THE MIND, LISTEN TO YOUR GUT

A first important step in rewiring the mind to trust your partner is to realize that there's nothing you can do to prevent them cheating on you or leaving you if they so desire. Your partner can do anything they want with anyone they want at any time. As unnerving as that may sound, it's also a liberating realization once you take it on board. When you realize that you can't control their actions by getting all emotional, and there's nothing you can do to prevent them leaving you, you begin to learn to trust. Granted, it can be hard to trust someone when you feel insecure but, in order to do it, you need to stop focusing on the "negative" aspects of their character, like their preference for friends of the opposite sex rather than the same sex, and instead concentrate on the positive aspects, like the fact they're happy with you now.

When suffering from jealousy in a relationship, the ego has an uncanny ability to completely make things up and present them as literal facts. It wants you to resist trusting your partner because it's been alerted to the "danger" of their sexual history, their flirtatiousness, or friendship with someone of the opposite sex. In reality, this is nonsense, and it's time you stopped listening to your mind and listening to your gut. In other words, if your partner is saying they want to be with you and no one else, then you need to trust that they mean it. If they're saying they love you, then you need to believe it. If they're acting and talking like they're happy with you and have no intention of cheating on you, then you need to let go and just trust that they're telling you the truth. You really have no other choice if you ever want peace of mind.

Again, this can be hard for a sufferer of relationship jealousy, as I know only too well. Emma wrote me love letters and was constantly reassuring me everything was okay, but none of it seemed to make much difference. I still preferred to focus on the negative side of things—her partying and male best friend. But once I made the conscious decision to listen to what she (and my gut) said, instead of my mind, I began to learn how to trust her.

Once you start to relax, and let go of your suspicions, you'll start to realize even more fully that these repeated thoughts and images are just manifestations in your mind of your worst fears, but they're far from accurate. Of course, there are no guarantees that your partner *won't* sleep with someone else at some point in the future, but unless they're giving you reason to believe it's a strong possibility, *you have to give them the benefit of the doubt.* Otherwise, you're just lost in a sea of suspicion, worrying about things that will probably never happen.

THE GRAND ILLUSION

We all have free will, right? Or do we? While it may feel like we're all free to think and do whatever we choose at any given moment, just how true is this? Are all of our choices in life completely within our control? Just how much free will do we really have? Without getting too deep into neuroscientific theory, the majority of scientists now believe that our sense of free will is in fact an illusion. Sam Harris, a philosopher and neuroscientist, puts it like this:

"The fact that our choices depend on prior cause does not mean that choice doesn't matter. To sit back and see what happens is also a choice that has its own consequences. So, the choices we make in life are as important as people think, but the next choice you make will come out of a wilderness of prior causes that you cannot see and did not bring into being."

In other words, the feeling that we're controlling our thoughts and actions is merely an illusion. We may think we're in control of them but in reality we're not. It's a myth. You may feel like you're making a conscious decision when you decide to buy a particular album, or date a particular person, or select sweet over salted popcorn at the movies, but most scientists would now agree that you're not. It has been scientifically proven that every so-called decision we make—from who to marry, to which pizza topping to go for—are not really arrived at by "us" but via a whole host of brain activities that we're not even aware of. (I'm no scientist, so please check out the

Resources Toolkit for a more robust explanation of "brain activities.")

If our thoughts precede our actions, then we should have free will in order to manipulate our actions by choosing our thoughts. But we don't. Instead, we're unable to choose which thoughts pop into our heads. An example of this is the "think of a movie star" question. Who pops into your consciousness when I ask you to think of an actor? Got someone? Good. So, how and why did you think of this person and *not* Sam Rockwell? Did you "choose" for them to appear, or did they just appear like magic out of your subconscious? Therefore, if we're not the author of our thoughts, how can we really in any sense regard ourselves as having free will?

This applies not only to small choices but larger ones too—to things like why you prefer certain foods, clothes, or TV programs over others, and to why you're attracted to certain people over others. For example, I love Thomas Hardy novels and yet can't stand Jane Austen. Am I *choosing* to feel this way? Or is there just something within me that means I can read *Tess of the D'Urbervilles* fifteen times and yet can't get past the first chapter of *Pride and Prejudice* without slipping into a coma? I didn't *choose* this aspect of my personal tastes, it just "is." And the same applies to you.

FREE WILL AND LETTING GO OF JEALOUSY

The knowledge that we don't have free will can help tremendously when it comes to overcoming relationship jealousy. To suffer from jealousy often means to judge our partner and feel that they "shouldn't behave as they do."

We love to:

- begrudge their past behavior
- begrudge their present behavior
- look down on them
- resent their keeping in touch with ex-lovers

But do they really have the freedom to do otherwise? If we're all just acting on the whim of our genes and neurons, can you really judge your partner's decisions? Whatever you're feeling angry, jealous and judgmental about, is simply being based on a variety of factors going on in your partner—their brain, genes, upbringing, society, life experience, and so on. Given these factors, it's slightly nonsensical to now judge the fact that they don't somehow make different choices that you'd prefer.

If we're all just acting on the whim of the neurons flying around in our brain, can we really *choose* to behave any differently? The truth is, we don't have half as much control over our thoughts and actions as we maybe think we do. And this should help tremendously in your fight to learn how to get over your jealousy. Just listen to your friend the next time he/she calls you with a hangover saying they didn't know "what they were thinking last night." Knowing this will make you see your partner in a new light as you begin to realize they're not as 100 percent responsible for their actions as you may have thought.

STEP SEVEN

EVERYTHING IS BECAUSE IT WAS

"The encounter could create a time paradox, the results of which could cause a chain reaction that would unravel the very fabric of the space time continuum, and destroy the entire universe!"
– Emmett L. "Doc" Brown

Although I dislike the phrase "everything happens for a reason"—as it implies we're all bound by fate, karma and all that stuff—it is true to a certain extent. Okay, there is no "reason" you and your partner were meant to find each other. There was no masterly grand design that brought you two together, but there was a chain of events, stretching way back before you were even aware of each other's existence, that led you to eventually meet. In short, your partner has made a series of big and small decisions throughout their life that has led them to where they are today. If they hadn't decided to go to that college, move to that town, start that job, etc. there's a strong possibility they wouldn't be with you now.

Naturally, a big part of that chain of events also includes their love life—the people they met, befriended, and dated. However, jealousy somehow conspires to make you upset and angry about the very people in your partner's life when you should actually be *glad* they met them. The reason why you should be glad they met becomes clear if you consider the question: If your partner had never befriended that person at X point in history, would they have met you? If they hadn't been with that particular girl or guy on those particular days in the past, maybe your paths would never have crossed.

So, as much as you might "hate" your partner's friendship with that guy or girl, would you want to change anything about it if you could, and risk messing with the space-time-continuum so there'd be a chance you don't even meet? Probably not. Therefore, learn to embrace the fact your partner knows the people they do and met them at the time they did because they played a pretty big part in bringing them to you.

Now, if you're hung up on the friendships your partner has maintained with people from their past—i.e. ex-lovers who are now just friends—another factor to consider here is the notion that they may well have gotten some things out of their system in this period they were single and fancy free. Using Emma as an example, the "promiscuous phase" I was so hung up about came right after leaving a long-term boyfriend. Like most people who've just come out of a big relationship, she'd simply felt the need to spend some time enjoying the single life and having casual relationships with different people. But while suffering from jealousy, I couldn't see that if she hadn't had those experiences when she was single before we met, she probably wouldn't have been ready to enter into a relationship with me in the first place.

The truth is, wanting your partner's past to be different means you're dissatisfied with it and, consequently, somehow with them. You think that "things just shouldn't have happened the way they did," but this is just your ego telling you you're "right" and they're "wrong" when it comes to their past. The truth is, like with everything connected with the ego, this is a false perspective. In reality, it turns out to have been *very important* that your partner met the people they did when they did. It's time to stop thinking of your partner's past as some kind of horrible period in history, which makes you feel threatened and angry and time to realize that everything that has happened *has happened perfectly.* If anything, you owe these ex-lovers and present friends a drink!

STEP EIGHT

THEIR LIFE, THEIR CHOICE

"Sex between two people is a beautiful thing; between five it's fantastic."
– Woody Allen

This step is specifically for those of you who are hung up about their partner's sexual history—people they're friends with, or still in contact with now, who've they've been intimate with in the past. So, if you couldn't care less about your partner's one-night-stands-turned-friends, or former friends-with-benefits, this step may not have as much meaning for you. For those of you who are freaked out about your partner's sex life before they met you, however, keep reading.

As you probably know, the reason why you're so hung up about your partner's relationship with someone they've slept with, is because you're being judgmental about sex. I know I've already covered how to stop being judgmental, but I think it's worth looking specifically at how to rewire the mind to stop being hung up about sex as it's a problem so permissive within sufferers of relationship jealousy.

How do we rewire the mind in this way? This can be done by realizing the truths contained within the following sub-headings on a profound, subconscious level. Really take the following concepts on board, let them sink deep into your subconscious and you'll feel your judgmental attitude about sex start to lift, and consequently your jealousy also.

THE MOST NATURAL THING IN THE WORLD

If you want to get a real handle on your relationship jealousy, you need to forget a lot of the nonsense we're brought up to believe about human sexuality. Unless you've been brought up in a strict religious household, the only reason why you're being so judgmental is because you're buying into societal "norms" that tell us that men and (especially) women, shouldn't "sleep around." Here lies a big reason why you're so disturbed by your partner's past sexual encounter or relationship with their friend—you're not seeing human sexuality in a clear, realistic, light.

This is why it doesn't matter how many times your partner says, "But I love you now," or, "The sex is so much better with you than them," because it's the fact that they did these things in the first place that burns you up. This is pure judgment. By viewing your partner's past sexual encounter or relationship as "bad," you're actually viewing them in a negative light also—that of a promiscuous sexaholic who may leave you at the drop of a hat for the first Jennifer Lawrence or Boris Kodjoe look-a-like who comes their way. Which, of course, is all in your mind. In reality, you need to think of your partner's past with their friend as being just being a normal part of them being alive.

If you're a guy, it's important to realize that women love sex just as much as men. This whole concept of women not being allowed to have as much sex, or enjoy sex as much as men, is merely a societal construct. There are dozens of reasons why your partner might have had casual sex in the past, including wanting to boost self-confidence, boost their mood, or to simply enjoy themselves. Can you honestly put your hand on your heart and say there's anything "wrong" with that? Or that you'd have turned down the same comparative sexual encounters your partner engaged in if they'd be presented to you?

Everyone occasionally engages in a variety of sexual acts for a wide variety of reasons. In most cases, if your partner was "sleeping around" they were probably single. Maybe they'd just broken up with someone and were feeling lonely. Maybe they were young and wanted to experiment. Maybe they just wanted to *have fun*. Imagine for a moment you're on trial for being too jealous of your partner's ex-lovers.

Would you really be able to stand up in front of a judge and jury and state in your defense: "I don't like the fact she had fun in the past. And she had fun by having sex, but women aren't supposed to enjoy that sort of thing." I hope you're beginning to see how ridiculous this mindset is.

Whatever the reason for your partner indulging in whatever sexual experiences in the past, understand that they had a right to those choices and they were completely natural choices *given their situation at the time*. Of course, if your partner was sleeping around with random people while supposedly in a serious relationship, then this may be cause for concern. If this is the case, you may want to ask them what motivated them to cheat on their ex. Chances are, though, they were single, and therefore free to do whatever they wanted.

SOME SCIENCEY STUFF

Here's a good question to ask yourself: Can you name one person you know, or have ever known, who *doesn't* like sex? Someone who might occasionally be attracted to certain people, but would never actually want to have sex with any of them? Someone who is yet to do anything more racy with another person than exchange a kiss on the cheek? If you can, there's a good chance they're asexual. Only roughly 1 percent of the world's population are asexual. Everyone else—that is, billions and billions of adults—*love* having sex.

Scientifically, sex can be viewed as a strong but subconscious urge to make ourselves feel better. Not just in the twenty minutes of sex (or one, depending on the partner), but emotionally and physically as a person. Countless studies have shown that sex produces various health benefits that most people aren't even aware of, but that subconsciously fuel our desire to have sex when we can. These range from better sleep patterns, to lower stress levels and blood pressure, and increased immunity. All in all, humans need sex, almost as much as they need food and water.

In his influential book, *Think and Grow Rich*, Napoleon Hill states that: "*As a therapeutic agency, sex has no equal.*" He goes on to say:

"Sexual desire is the most powerful of human desires. When driven by this desire, people develop keenness of imagination, courage, willpower, persistence and creative ability unknown to them at other times. So strong and impelling is the desire

for sexual contact that people freely run the risk of life and reputation to indulge it."

So, it's time to lighten up, stop taking sex so seriously and stop being so judgmental. Sex is really not such a big deal if you think about it in terms of a basic human function. The only reason why it seems such a big deal is because we, as a society, have made it into one. In reality, it can be viewed as merely a simple human urge and it helps greatly to view the sex your partner had in the past as a mechanical function, rather than an emotional function. Think of it as a necessary process—something they were wired to do by evolution in order to feel better—rather than as an unnecessary "dirty" desire that should've been avoided.

Also, it's very beneficial to remember that whatever sex they had in the past certainly didn't change their life, or enlighten them in any way. *No* sex is that great. The chances are very high that it wasn't some kind of earth shattering event in which they forged an amazing connection with the other person and which both of them will never forget. The truth is more likely that they just experienced it and quickly moved on. Always, always, always remember: If your partner didn't enjoy sex in general, they wouldn't enjoy it with you. And if they didn't like girls/guys, *they wouldn't even be with you.*

I have been asked in the past, however, in an email:

"Isn't it hard to lighten up about sex if it's something so powerful, personal, and intimate? Aren't we just kidding ourselves if we think sex between two people isn't a very intimate experience?"

To this I would say, no. The fact that sexual desire is so pervasive means it's *easy* to lighten up about it. I think the problem some people have is that they confuse Napoleon Hill's definition of sex with their own interpretation of sex.

Napoleon Hill merely states that sexual desire is one of the most powerful of human desires—a primal want and need—but he doesn't say anything about it being "personal" or "intimate." And that's my point: Sex *is* a powerful human desire, but this means that it's also just a basic human need, rather than an indicator of close personal intimacy. The need for sex is hardwired into all of us, negating the notion that something "magical" has to be going on between two people in order for them to have sex. In other words, the fact your partner had casual sex with someone else in the past is probably more indicative of their basic human need for sex—with a half decent mate—rather than wanting to be close, personal and intimate with him or her in particular.

It's time to realize that what *you* have with your partner—commitment, real intimacy, love, friendship, etc.—far outweigh the fleeting moments of instant gratification found in mere sex. A connection like the one you have with your partner is something these ex-lovers probably never had.

OUR MEMORY SUCKS

We tend to talk about memory like it's a "thing" that exists in our heads—a compartment in our brain—when in reality it's a just concept. Your partner may have memories of their past, but they don't really exist as "things" that are somehow permanently lodged in their mind. The truth is, our memories are pretty pathetic. Scientists have only a vague idea of how memories are stored and recalled, but what they all agree on is that the whole process is a bit of a mess. They fade considerably over time until they're virtually unrecognizable from the original moment.

What can you really remember about an experience you had with a lover in the past? Can you remember what they were wearing? What music was playing? What the weather was like? You might have a very vague recollection of some of these things, but I'm thinking unless it was last week, or you have a super retentive memory, it's not much more than that.

And that's the sum total of what still exists in your partner's mind—vague, hazy recollections about a distant event that's growing hazier and hazier by the day. Your jealously should begin to further subside once you realize you're getting hung up on an event in the past which your partner can hardly remember themselves and which no longer exists.

PART III

LET'S GET PRACTICAL

STEP NINE

WAIT. STOP. DON'T GO THERE

"Jealousy is, I think, the worst of all faults because it makes a victim of both parties."
– Gene Tierney

This first step in this section is not actually about doing certain actions every day, but about *stopping* certain actions every day. When you get anxious, upset and angry about your partner talking to or being friends with someone of the opposite sex, you're letting your ego define how you react to it. And often this means spending hours trying to figure out why you're feeling the way you do and/or invading your partner's personal space.

So, if you are indulging your ego by doing any of the four things below, you need to eliminate them from your behavior immediately!

STOP TRAWLING

As you may have gathered, part of the reason why you suffer from relationship jealousy in the first place is because you've spent so long trying to figure out the answer for yourself. As previously mentioned, the mind loves getting its teeth into seemingly unsolvable problems. The very process of trying to fathom why you're feeling the way you do about your partner's behavior, and to work out a solution, is part of what's keeping your jealousy alive.

I can remember spending hours Googling, "Stop being jealous of girlfriend's friend," "Overcome jealousy in a relationship," etc. and always, without fail, feeling worse at the end of each session than I did at the beginning. Trust me, it's not helping. It's only making things worse. And besides, you now have this book. However, even this book should not be re-read more than is absolutely necessary. By reading and thinking about jealousy, you are inadvertently keeping it fresh in your mind and feeding the monster.

STOP SNOOPING

If you've ever snooped around your partner's Facebook account, emails or phone, or been tempted to, this section's for you. Perversely, the one thing you fear and hate the most, you also have a morbid curiosity for. You want to know more about the situation in the hope you'll hear what you want to hear and will somehow feel better afterwards. Of course, it doesn't work quite like that, and finding out more information usually only adds more fuel to the fire, making your jealousy even worse.

This curiosity to find things out, though, can lead down very dangerous paths. Not only does it, in all likelihood, make you feel one hundred times worse than before, but you also run the risk of getting caught and seriously undermining the relationship. Plus, it shows a major lack of respect for your partner's privacy, which isn't a good thing at all. So, whenever you feel the urge to go take a look through their phone or laptop, *force yourself* to resist it at all costs. This is an absolutely crucial step in getting over relationship jealousy, because if you're unable to resist it means you're still being controlled by your ego and have a great deal of work left to do.

STOP QUIZZING

This is a big one. I have no idea why so many people give the opposite advice, but you must resist at all costs the urge to "talk it out" with your partner. This is about you, not them.

You think that by asking questions you may hear what you want to hear, and then your jealousy will magically disappear. You want to hear "He's not as good looking as you," or, "She was so boring I used to fall asleep with my eyes open," but, sadly, it doesn't work like that. Even if you do hear what you think you want to hear, it won't make you feel any better. There's absolutely nothing your partner can say or do that will suddenly turn off the jealous monkey chatter flying around your head. This is because it's not your partner's actions that are the problem, it's your lack of confidence.

Discussing your jealousy with your partner is never a good idea. One, because before you know it, half an hour has gone by wasted discussing about their "standards." And two, because asking questions and letting your partner know how you're feeling makes you look insecure, and no one finds insecurity attractive. It signals to your partner that you lack a certain amount of confidence in yourself and that's why you're asking all these silly questions. In reality, one of the most valued qualities both men and women look for in a partner is confidence.

STOP DWELLING

The only reason you're suffering from this condition is because to some extent you're *choosing* to give a disproportionate amount of "mind space" to it. Think about it: If you never allowed yourself to become embroiled in endless ruminations about your partner's potentially cheating behavior, would you technically still suffer from relationship jealousy?

Once you stop thinking about it all the time, you'll stop acting on these thoughts. Many might say though, "Okay, but I can't *help* thinking about it. What do I do?" This is true to a point— you can't control the random thoughts that pop into and out of your head, whether they're jealous ones or not, but you *can* control whether you choose to dwell on these thoughts. You can choose to stop yourself from focusing on your jealousy while sitting on the bus, lying in bed at night or wherever you are, if you wish. Granted this can be hard, but it's not impossible.

Thoughts and emotions about your partner's real and imagined behavior are inextricably linked, but there is a specific process that's occurring every time you succumb to relationship jealousy. This exercise will help you step away from this downward spiral of thoughts and emotions and, over time, break the so-called "power" they have over you.

Let's start by taking a look at what this downward spiral entails:

1. A jealous thought pops in the mind
2. A jealous emotion appears in the body
3. A cycle of repetitive jealous thoughts and emotions begins

The gap between each stage may be a micro-second, but it's impossible to feel jealous, angry, or any emotion at all without first thinking about it. All emotions can be physically felt in the body—and from here it's all too easy to spiral down into a vicious circle of overthinking and overreacting.

Here's the three-step process you should follow to stop this happening:

1. Become Aware Of The Thoughts And Emotions. You can't prevent these jealous thoughts and emotions from popping up in your brain and body, but you *can* control how you choose to react to them. When thoughts and emotions about the past arise, simply notice them. Take a step back and disassociate yourself from them by recognizing them as merely impressions and sensations. And without judgment or resistance.

2. Replace With Positive Thoughts And Emotions. Now conjure up an image in your mind of you and your partner together, happy and in love. (It might be a good idea to select a photo beforehand so your mind has an image ready at hand.) As you recall this image, really feel the love you two share. Let all the negative, jealous thoughts and emotions about your partner with someone from the past, become overwhelmed by thoughts and emotions of the love you share with your partner. Doing this removes you from your jealous state and grounds you once again in the present moment. It creates a gap in which your mind is able to recognize the difference between what's real: your relationship. And what's not: your mind hallucinations.

After months and months of trying various techniques to rid myself of jealous thoughts and emotions as they appeared, I found that this technique worked best of all. By far. I'm not saying it's easy but, as Beverly Sills once said, "There are no shortcuts to any place worth going." And once you've mastered it, you'll feel like nothing can touch you. Over time you should begin to feel less and less of an emotional reaction every time you have a jealous thought, and finally they'll just pop in and out of your mind like any other inconsequential thought. You *can* do it if you really want to. Just don't allow your mind to go down that jealousy road, and do whatever you can to wrench it back into the present moment.

Often, to suffer from relationship jealousy means that you're maybe not being as productive as you could be in your day to day life, and so are feeling unchallenged or unfulfilled in some way. Remember, the mind *loves* to be kept occupied by challenges, and so if you don't provide any it'll just go ahead and make up imaginary ones instead. So, if you're stuck in a boring job, or are unemployed, or feel lost in some way generally, these are all perfect breeding grounds for negative, meaningless thoughts to fester.

On the other hand, if you're fully engaged in life, have a hobby or job that interests and excites you, have a great set of friends or family, and are generally engaged in regular activities that give you a sense of purpose, it's much harder for the mind to become embroiled in meaningless pursuits such as creating imaginary problems in your relationship.

STEP TEN

PUT OUT THE FIRE

"Empty your mind. Be formless, shapeless, like water."
– Bruce Lee

Regular mediation has been scientifically proven to reduce the stress generated by the brain's amygdala. It reduces the chances of getting certain diseases, as well as improving cognitive functioning and a host of other benefits. So, if you're not already meditating, now might be a good time to start, as it helps prevent the mind from racing backwards and forwards in time and trains it to just observe what's happening in the present. And the present moment is, of course, exactly where you should be spending more time if you suffer from relationship jealousy.

The type of mediation I recommend is called "mindfulness," but you can choose whichever kind you like. In the Resources Toolkit you'll find plenty of options.

HOW TO PRACTICE MINDFULNESS IN 3 STEPS

Find a quiet place to sit or lie down. Make sure you're alone and won't be disturbed. Set an alarm to go off in ten minutes, and then follow these three steps. (Leave your eyes open or closed, whichever you prefer.)

1. Take five deep breaths and relax every muscle in your body from your head to your toes.

2. Simply become of what's happening around and within you, moment-by-moment and non-judgmentally. Focus on the present moment. The here and now. Concentrate on your breathing, or how your body feels in the chair. Listen to sounds in the room. Look at the patterns on the wallpaper etc. Just observe whatever's happening, as it happens.

3. When you find that your mind has drifted away and become lost in thought, simply acknowledge it without judgment. Then return your attention to something in the external rather than internal world—your breathing, the sounds outside, a breeze etc.

And that's all there is to it. I found twenty minutes meditation a day worked best for me, but some people like to do it for just five minutes, and some for an hour. I suggest starting with ten minutes and then working your way up to twenty minutes or half an hour a day. You can choose any of the mediation methods out there but if you've never practiced it before I highly recommend starting with a "guided meditation," i.e. listening to someone talk you through it on a pre-recorded track. Sam Harris's guided mediation included in the Resources Toolkit is really great, and I found listening to the twenty-five minute version every day worked perfectly for me when I first started out.

Now, I remember trying to meditate in the past and it didn't seem to work. It felt like I was just staring at a wall and nothing seemed to happen—I was just thinking about things as I usually do. And this went on for weeks. This is perfectly normal for beginners, but will pass. It can be hard to know when you're doing it "right" at first, and the simple answer is— if you feel a sense of calm after meditating and in your life in general, then it's working. While you're actually meditating, however, you'll know when you're doing it "right" when you're able to just observe whatever's happening around you (including your own thoughts) with ease. Over time the struggle to meditate and "not think" relaxes and it becomes easier to slip into a meditative state of pure awareness. You may even experience a "breakthrough meditation" session like I did, in which you find yourself laughing with joy for no apparent reason. It was pretty strange, but also wonderful and

I knew I'd reached a point where I could comfortably say I knew how to meditate.

What also helped me learn how to meditate was discovering that I was literally triggering a "relaxation nerve" in my brain called the vagus nerve. This nerve runs from your brain, via the heart and lungs, all the way down to the abdomen. When this nerve is stimulated through deep breathing, the amygdala in your brain calms down and "the fire" is put out. Do this regularly enough and it will help the amygdala stop flaring up in the first place. Relationship jealousy is simply a stressful reaction in the amygdala to the circumstances surrounding your relationship, and when I realized that I was fighting it by stimulating a nerve, I took the whole process more seriously and was able to reap the benefits more easily.

THE EGO VS. YOUR TRUE SELF

I've mentioned a few times in this book the concept of the ego being responsible for your negative and jealous thoughts, rather than your true self. Well, meditation is the key to beginning to see this more clearly. By making you more aware of the present moment, meditation forces you to become more attuned to your true self. It forces you to get in touch with that part of you that simply observes experience (including thought) as it happens, rather than analyze it, critique it and judge it through the lens of the ego.

A good analogy to explain this is to equate our thoughts as cars whizzing by on a busy street. Imagine each car is a thought that comes and goes. It appears, and it disappears as quickly as it arrived. Now imagine that you're standing in the middle of the street and the cars/thoughts are whizzing by in both directions. Now start to float up above the street, and so you're now looking down on the cars coming and going. This is akin to meditating and being in the state of your true self. You are now looking down and observing your thoughts, but you're not down on the ground experiencing them. You're simply watching them go by. The ego tricks you into believing that you *are* your thoughts and emotions, and that you identify with them. Meditation opens up the reality that you are not your thoughts or emotions because if you're witnessing them, how can they be "you"? You are, in fact, the awareness that's doing the witnessing.

ALL WE HAVE IS NOW

In essence, both the past and the future are illusions. The past has already been and gone, and the future is yet to arrive, and so what are we left with? *The right here and now.* It may seem an obvious point to make, but is it possible to do anything outside of the now? Are you able to make a single action, or think a single thought that happens in the past or the future? No. But when suffering from relationship jealousy this fundamental truth seems to somehow slip by the wayside.

Instead, you "hate" your partner's past or present behavior, despite the fact that it doesn't exist in any meaningful sense.

When you're thinking about your relationship and getting all queasy about it, it's important to remember that you're actually thinking about an hallucination created by your mind in the present, rather than something that actually exists anywhere outside of your own head. If we look at life as a series of experiences, moment by moment, meditation is the means by which we are able to fully realize this, and to have the chance to not worry about anything, because nothing's threatening us in the present moment. Your partner is not thinking about their ex lover. They are not in love with someone at work, and have no desire to leave you. Through meditation, we are able to better tap into the fact that the past and future don't exist and nothing can hurt us in the present moment—certainly not mere thoughts.

STEP ELEVEN

PUT ON THEIR SHOES

"Life is all memory, except for the one present moment that goes by you so quickly you hardly catch it going."
– Tennessee Williams

A FRIEND TEST

If your jealousy is centered on your partner's friendship with someone of the opposite sex, I want you to write down at the top of a sheet of paper the name of someone you're friends with of the opposite sex. If you don't have any friends like this, just choose someone from your past. Have a think about this person for a minute or two. What are they like? What's your relationship like with them?

Then, underneath the name, answer the following questions:

1. What do you feel when you think about this person? Romantic feelings or friendship?

2. Compared to your relationship with your partner, is this relationship a) Definitely more important, b) As important, c) Nowhere near as important.

3. How often would you say you think about this person and your shared experiences? a) Often, b) Occasionally, c) Hardly ever.

And that's it.

I'm guessing the answers you gave go something like this:

1. Friendship.

2. "c."

3. "c", or maybe "b."

Well, that's *exactly* how much your partner's "best" friend means to them: nothing compared to you.

BEFRIEND YOUR PARTNER'S FRIENDS

Now it's time to put the results of this test into practice. In order to overcome this jealousy you have of specific and/or random people in your partner's life, you need to start conjuring up different emotions to the ones you're feeling at the moment when you think about them. You need to take all of those feelings of disgust, anger and bitterness that's built up inside you toward them, and turn them into feelings of positivity, peace and even, dare I say it, friendship.

I remember how I used to feel whenever I thought about Emma's friend, Jack. I didn't like him *at all*. Whenever I'd see or hear the name Jack anywhere—on TV, in a newspaper, or online I'd be overcome by a wave of nausea. (It was around this time incidentally that I began to realize just how many characters in Hollywood movies are called Jack.) Basically whenever I thought of this guy, I felt very, very negatively toward him. I imagined that if I met him at party or something, I'd probably cause a big embarrassing scene. But then I began to realize that this attitude was getting me absolutely nowhere. All I was doing was churning up completely nonsensical animosity toward a guy I didn't even know, and making myself constantly angry and anxious for no real fathomable reason. Instead, I learned how to start "liking" him in my mind by thinking of him as a friend rather than a foe.

Here's what I did: I purposefully set out to get to know him. Instead of avoiding situations in which I might meet him, I deliberately set out to meet him as often as possible. After a while, a funny thing began to happen… I actually began to get along with him. Okay, maybe not in a best bud kind of way, but I began to think of him as a guy I kind of liked and respected. This enabled me to deliberately reframe my image of him as this terrible guy—with the temerity to pester my girlfriend whenever he felt like it!—into just a regular guy. A guy just trying to have some fun in this life. A guy with his own set of hang ups. A guy who liked movies and football, etc. In short, a guy I may have been friends with anyway if I'd met him under other circumstances.

A very strange thing started to happen once I made the conscious effort to do this. I stopped feeling bitter, angry and resentful toward Jack and her other male friends, and started seeing them just as people. After all, if you think about it, what do you really have to be angry with these friends about? Aren't they the people who are in a way responsible for you two meeting in the first place, in terms of the space time continuum? If they're ex-lovers, aren't they the people who let your partner get all of their "playing the field" experiences out of the way? If they're ex-boyfriends or girlfriends, aren't they the people who helped your partner grow as a person?

Give it go. Next time your partner goes out with a friend you don't like, ask to go with them. Make a point of getting to know this friend and observe how they interact with your partner. It may not be easy at first, but practice it and you should find that it helps alleviate some of the anxiety you have coursing around inside you about their relationship. It will teach you to be happy in the moment, and in the knowledge that your partner has rejected every other person like this they've ever met, and chosen to be with you instead.

STEP TWELVE

CHOOSE HAPPINESS

"What I used to be will pass away, and then you'll see that all I want now is happiness for you and me."
– Elliott Smith

I can safely say that the following three exercises were the ones that really helped me seal the deal in beating my relationship jealousy. I had been going through a back and forth period of feeling better about things, and then not so good, but these exercises really killed off any lingering feelings of jealousy still knocking around in my head. I hope they do the same for you.

PART I: MAKE A COMMITMENT

This may sound too simple to be effective, but you need to actually make a conscious commitment to forgo all of the negative emotions that have built up inside you—stress, anxiety, judgment, suspicion, anger—in favor of happiness. It's time to simply *choose happiness*. By this I mean that you need to decide that from this day on, that you're going to really try to just look at the positive side of your relationship, rather than the negative. Focus on the fact that you're together and in love, rather than whatever they might or might not do in the future.

I realize this may sound too simple, and maybe similar to what you've already been told along the lines of "just get over it," but this is different. It's different if you consider that how we choose to think about *all* of our situations in life goes a long way to determining how we actually cope with them. You may not believe it right now, but you are choosing to some extent to react with fear and judgement rather than with rationality. Now is the time to just let it go and be more like the duck I mentioned in the beginning of this book. Learn to shake the water off your back, and move on. This takes perseverance, of course, but here are two practical steps you can do every day that will help you get there.

PART II: MORNING EXERCISE

Every morning from now on, I want you to do the following when you wake up: Stop to consider for a moment *just how good you've actually got it*. If you actually think about it, you're pretty lucky. You have so much going for you in the here and now, but rather than realize this, you're choosing instead at the moment to dwell on imaginary threats.

Here are the kind of thoughts I want you to think about and/or write down each morning when you wake up:

- It's amazing that I met my partner in the first place. I'm so happy we happened to be on that train/in that bar/taking that class, on Match.com, etc. at the same time.

- And now I'm actually in a relationship. Not everyone can say that. Being eternally single is the bane of many people I know, and most would probably do anything to be in my position.

- Even people who are in relationships aren't always happy, but I'm in a relationship with someone who loves me, and I love them.

- If I think about it, I've got a great thing going on here. My mind is just creating problems where there are none.

- What do I really have to be unhappy about? Is my partner really thinking about someone else all the time? No. Are they talking about them all the time? No. Are they in love with you? Yes. Therefore, I should just smile and choose to *be happy*.

PART III: NIGHT EXERCISE

Furthering on from that exercise, every night before you go to bed, I want you to do the following:

Grab your notepad and simply make a list of three things that went well, or you enjoyed, during the day. (It's best to write them down rather than simply think about them.) Just jot down three things which brought a smile to your face, whether they were big or small. They don't have to be out of the ordinary, amazing things like, "I bumped into [insert favorite celebrity's name] walking down the street." Rather, put down the simple things that made you happy in a small way, like, I had an amazing slice of cake at Starbucks. Or, I had a great, funny conversation with Suzy this afternoon about UFOs. Doing this has been scientifically proven to make people appreciate what they have more, and their lives in general.

The three points also don't necessarily have to be about your partner, but if they are—great! The point, though, is to begin to recalibrate your mind into appreciating the smaller things in life again, whether they involve your partner or not. In fact, both the morning and night exercises are designed to do just that—make you see that what you have is actually pretty amazing, if you'd only stop to think about it once in a while, rather than keep obsessing over "negative" things. So, do both exercises morning and night for two weeks and see how you feel by the end of it. I can guarantee you'll soon feel so much better than you do now.

THE TWO BEST MEDICINES

I want you to do these four things, right now. Don't worry, I'll wait for you.

1. Give your current state of retroactive jealousy a number: 1 being the lowest and 10 the highest.

2. Watch this video: Go to YouTube and put "Boomerang presenter can't stop laughing" in the search field.

3. Listen to this song at full volume: Stay on YouTube and run a search for the song *You Get What You Give* by the New Radicals. Listen to it at full volume.

4. **Repeat** step 1.

Was the last number you wrote down higher than the first? While you may think the effects of laughing at a funny video or listening to a feel-good song are temporary, here's the strange thing: *the more often you do it, the less temporary the effects.*

THE HEALING POWER OF LAUGHTER

You may not be aware of it but laughing does more for us than just providing us with temporary comic relief. In much the same way as having sex produces various health benefits—ranging from better sleep patterns, to lower stress levels and blood pressure, to increased immunity—laughing has a similar positive effect on the body.

In study after study it's been shown that laughter (and we're talking proper yuks here, not just some light giggling) causes an increase in a whole host of life enhancing properties, including:

- An increase in "natural killer cells" which attack viral infected cells, cancer and tumors
- An increase in activated T cells, which "turn up" the immune system
- An increase in the antibody IgA, which fights respiratory infections
- An increase in gamma interferon, which activates the immune system
- An increase in IgB, the immunoglobulin produced in the greatest quantity in body
- An increase in Complement 3, which helps antibodies to pierce dysfunctional or infected cells

Laughing's great for the fighting dysfunctional cells and the immune system, but studies have also shown that it's also good at decreasing stress hormones, dopamine levels and consequently blood pressure. Again, much like sex, laughter is a form of aerobic workout which increases the body's oxygen functioning.

Scientists even believe that when employed alongside conventional care, the positive emotions released by laughter help reduce pain and aid in the healing of diseases. Here's Norman Cousins, the man who "cured himself of disease through the power of laughter" on the subject:

"I made the joyous discovery that ten minutes of genuine belly laughter had an anesthetic effect and would give me at least two hours of pain-free sleep. When the pain-killing effect of the laughter wore off, my wife and I would switch on the motion picture projector again and not infrequently, it would lead to another pain-free interval."

Way back in 1964, Cousins was given just a few months left to live after being diagnosed with a rare degenerative disease known as Ankylosing Spondylitis. He was left in almost constant pain and was advised by his doctor advised to get his "affairs in order". Cousins, however, was never a man to turn down a challenge, and rather than draw up a will and wait for the inevitable, he instead drew up an action plan to beat the disease himself. The first casualty was his doctor, who was promptly fired and replaced with one who wouldn't interfere as much.

Next, he moved out of hospital and into a hotel, whereupon he set up a movie projector and began administering a high daily dosage of Marx Brothers movies direct to his funny bone. (Luckily, Cousins was unable to get hold of any *Carry On* movies or he probably wouldn't have survived the week.) His condition steadily improved and within a couple of months he was back on his feet. Two years later he was back at his job as editor-in-chief at the *Saturday Review.* He died in 1990—a full twenty-six years after being told by his doctor he wouldn't live to see Christmas.

It's impossible to tell, of course, whether Norman Cousin's recovery was solely due to Harpo's bicycle horn and Groucho's put-downs. He also took high does of vitamin C, was generally an optimistic person, and perhaps most importantly, left the hospital—somewhere he called "no place for a person who is seriously ill." But there's no doubt that laughter strengthens the immune system that fights disease, elevates the mood and releases positive emotions. And that can only be a good thing when it comes to getting over retroactive jealousy.

THE HEALING POWER OF MUSIC

Everything you've just learned about the healing power of laughter can be applied to music. A ton of research has been done indicating that regular listening to (or playing) music is a potent treatment for all kinds of health issues, including depression, stress, anxiety, chronic pain and even schizophrenia. As with laugher, sex, and meditation, music does this by producing positive physical and biological changes which boost the immune system, reduce heart rate, blood pressure and cortisol levels. Finally, there also appears to be a link between music, happiness and pleasure. Hearing songs that we like stimulates the same "pleasure center" of the brain that makes us laugh, quaff down our favorite foods, or snort a line of coke. Not that I'm advocating the latter, of course, but you get the picture. Music can be used as a drug. Only less expensive and better for you.

When choosing what music to listen to, I'd recommend sticking to upbeat tracks with a positive message. Create a playlist of your favorite feel-good tunes and incorporate listening to at least three tracks into your daily routine.

ANTI-JEALOUSY PLAYLIST

Below you'll find a collection of some of the best relationship jealousy crushing songs around, curated from my record collection.

- **YouTube**: Put in "Jeff Billings Jealousy" and find the playlist on my YouTube channel.
- **Prescription**: Turn volume up to eleven. Dancing is optional, but advised.
- **Warning**: May create sudden feelings of happiness, renewed optimism and a lust for life. Use care when operating a car or dangerous machinery.

Here's the playlist:

01. Beyond The Sea – Bobby Darin
02. There'll Be Some Changes Made – Dave Brubeck
03. Success – Iggy Pop
04. Time To Pretend – MGMT
05. Energy – The Apples In Stereo
06. Whatever It Is – Ben Lee
07. The Boss – James Brown
08. Come Back Brighter – Reef
09. Doing All Right – Queen
10. All We Have Is Now – The Flaming Lips
11. There's A New World Just Opening For Me – The Kinks

12. Winner Of The… – Pavement

13. Beginning To See The Light – The Velvet Underground

14. The Line Is Fine – Travis

15. It Doesn't Matter Anymore – The Supernaturals

16. Don't You Worry 'Bout A Thing – Stevie Wonder

17. On A Plain – Nirvana

18. Happiness – Elliott Smith

19. Lay Back In The Sun – Spiritualized

20. Some Sweet Day – Sparklehorse

21. You Get What You Give – New Radicals

22. This Will Be My Year – Semisonic

23. This Will Be Our Year – The Zombies

24. Movin' On Up – Primal Scream

25. We're A Winner – The Impressions

26. Road To Joy – Bright Eyes

27. Nothing'severgonnastandinmyway (again) – Wilco

28. Ola Kala – I'm From Barcelona

29. Mr. Lucky – John Lee Hooker

30. You Can Have The World – Cameo

31. I'm So Free – Lou Reed

32. A Change Is Gonna Come? – The High Fidelity

33. Ain't That A Kick In The Head – Dean Martin

34. Feel So Good – The Brian Jonestown Massacre

35. Hand In My Pocket – Alanis Morrisette

36. Sing A Happy Song – The O'Jays

37. Lucky Number Nine – The Moldy Peaches

38. Non, Je Ne Regrette Rien – Edith Piaf

39. All The Wine – The National

40. Things Are Looking Up – Fred Astaire

41. Younger Yesterday – The Polyphonic Spree

42. Mr Blue Sky – Electric Light Orchestra

43. Getting Better – The Beatles

44. Roll With It – Oasis

45. Solid – The Dandy Warhols

46. It Doesn't Matter – The Chemical Brothers

47. I'm Sitting On Top Of The World – Al Jolson

48. Don't Stop – Fleetwood Mac

49. I'm Blessed – Brendan Benson

50. Keep Your Sunny Side Up – Jane Gaynor

51. Feelin' All Right – Len

52. Beautiful – Carol King

53. Dry The Rain – The Beta Band

54. Paris Sous La Neige – Mellow

55. Whatever Will Be, Will Be (Que Sera Sera) – Doris Day

56. Vagabond – Wolfmother

57. Beautiful – Athlete

58. And When The Morning Comes – Superstar

59. You Take Yourself Too Seriously – The Supernaturals

60. Raindrops Keep Falling On My Head – Andy Williams

61. Do It All Over Again – Spiritualized

62. The Classical – Pavement

63. Love What You Do – The Divine Comedy

64. Consideration – Reef

65. Singin' In The Rain – Gene Kelly

66. Lady Day And John Coltrane – Gil Scott-Heron

67. Big Indian – The Dandy Warhols

68. Mr E's Beautiful Blues – Eels

69. Bad Days – The Flaming Lips

70. Lovely Day – Bill Withers

71. What A Wonderful World – Louis Armstrong

72. You Can't Always Get What You Want – The Rolling Stones

73. Good Times Comin' My Way – The Lassie Foundation

74. The 59th Bridge Song (Feeling Groovy) – Simon & Garfunkel

75. Move On Up – Curtis Mayfield

76. Float On – Modest Mouse

77. Hey Man (Now You're Really Living) – Eels

78. Always Look On The Bright Side Of Life – Monty Python

79. Don't Worry, Be Happy – Bobby McFerrin

80. Smile – Nat "King" Cole

81. Baby, I'm A Star – Prince

82. Don't Stop Me Now – Queen

83. O-o-h Child – Nina Simone

84. Beautiful – Christina Aguilera

85. Everything Is AWESOME!!! – Lego Movie

86. Mother, We Just Can't Get Enough – New Radicals

87. I'm So Glad – Cream

YOU ALREADY HAVE IT ALL

There's a scene in one of my favorite movies, *Annie Hall*, in which Alvy explains his view of life to Annie:

"I feel that life is divided up into the horrible and the miserable, those are the two categories, y'know? The horrible would be like, I don't know, terminal cases like blind people, crippled… I don't know how they get through life, it's amazing to me. And the miserable is everyone else. So, when you go through life you should be thankful that you're miserable."

As Alvy says, maybe it's time to start being thankful that right now you're just miserable. Maybe your partner's past isn't quite how you'd like it to be, but do want to know how good your life is compared to the majority of the human race that's now living, *or has ever lived,* on this planet?

THINGS COULD ALWAYS BE WORSE

Have you heard of a guy called Nick Vujicic? He's a Serbian-Australian motivational speaker (and Christian evangelist, but nobody's perfect) who was born with Phocomelia—a rare disorder that causes severe birth defects, especially of the upper limbs. In Nick's case, this resulted in him being born with no arms and no legs. He's also happily married, successful and has a kid. Imagine you'd been born with no arms and no legs.

Or with one of the many other birth defects out there, such as dwarfism (failure to grow to normal size), ambras syndrome (excessive facial and body hair), progeria (excessive aging), and so on.

Imagine you'd been born, or had found yourself, in any one of the hundreds of "horrible" categories out there: blind, deaf, dumb, terminally ill, and so on. Or that you were born in the midst of a war zone, say in Africa or the Middle East, and every day's a struggle just to stay alive. Or that you've been convicted of a crime you didn't commit and sentenced to death. You wouldn't have the time or the head space to suffer from retroactive jealousy.

In 2016 there was much talk that it was "the worst year ever." This means it was worse than being hit by a plague outburst in the fourteenth century. Or living in an East End slum in 1880s London. Or being lined up and shot during one of Lenin, Hitler or Mao's purges. However, the list of genuinely worst circumstances you *could have* experienced due to sheer bad luck is endless. But right now you're living in the best time there's ever been to be alive. A time that billions upon billions of people now dead never had the chance to experience. *But you do*. And not only that, you have someone who loves you to share it with. So, whenever you sometimes feel like your life is crappy, monotonous or pointless, take a moment to remind yourself that maybe your life isn't as bad as you think it is. There are a million ways it could be worse. Much worse...

WHAT ARE THE ODDS?

13.7 billion years ago. A hot dense mass about the size of pea, bursts. The resulting colossal explosion of energy flings matter at an incomprehensible speed in all directions, billions of mile wide, creating the universe as we now know it. As the universe expands, energy cools and matter congeals into atoms. Gravity crushes them together causing them to ignite and form our solar system.

4.5 billion years ago. Clouds of dust, rocks and ice orbiting the newly formed sun, get pulled together by the force of gravity into one giant clump, forming Earth. Then, another planet smashes into Earth and the resulting debris clusters again under the force of gravity, forming the moon. This collision also tips the Earth onto its axis, giving us our four seasons. Microbial life—a kind of bacterium—appears in Earth's seas soon afterwards.

2.5 billion years ago. Photosynthesis is born when some microbial life forms living in the sea begin converting carbon dioxide in the air into food, using energy from the sun. This transforms Earth forever as oxygen gets pumped into the air— so much so that the sky turns from red to blue—and life explodes in complexity and variety as they harness the energy-giving properties in an oxygen rich atmosphere.

400 million years ago. Plant life and fungi successfully transition onto land.

250 — 220 million years ago. The Earth's landmasses converge to form one supercontinent. Mountains form when continents collide and earthquakes rip them apart. These teutonic shifts produce major climate changes, with the Earth tipping from very hot to very cold. Dinosaurs prove to be the most successful creatures to have ever existed, due to their ability to lay eggs inland and far from the sea. However, they are wiped out when a six mile wide asteroid slams into the Earth. Some mammals survive by taking to the water again and adapting back into life in the sea.

30 million years ago. Mammals migrate across the globe. Primates in Africa migrate to South America and eventually cross to Asia where they lose their tails, becoming apes.

3 million — 13,000 years ago. The first upright apes appear on the grassy plains of Africa and, roughly 1 million years later, begin using stone tools. Over the next 2 million years the brain size of humans increases substantially, probably due to increased hand-eye coordination, and they harness fire. Five-hundred-thousand years ago, neanderthals emerge, only to possibly be hunted to extinction by modern humans. Fifty-thousand years ago modern humans emerge in Africa, migrate across Europe and Asia reaching Australia about 40,000 years ago and the Americas about 13,000 years ago. Somewhere among these tribes of early humans, battling to survive against all the odds, are your direct descendants. And so begins another stage in the billions of events that led directly to you being born...

Apologies for the history lesson, but given these remarkable series of events what do you think were the odds that you'd even be born? (Let alone be lucky enough to meet your partner.) Turns out it's quite a big number—roughly one in 400 TRILLION. That's basically an unfathomable number of events that had to occur—from the Big Bang itself, to Earth being formed, to homo sapiens emerging victorious over every other species of human, to your parents meeting in a disco in 1968—in order for you to actually arrive in this world. Think about this for a moment. It's INCREDIBLE.

I realize, of course, that it's not always useful to put the cart before the horse in these situations. If you were to throw a can of paint at a large canvas hanging on a wall, the chances of the paint landing exactly where it did is probably also one in 400 trillion. There were no odds involved—the paint just happened to land where it did. And the same is true of your chances of being born. You're not here on this planet because of chance and odds, but because a random, yet causal chain of events has occurred, resulting in you being here. There's only one of you that's ever walked this Earth and there's only ever going to be one of you after you've gone, and that's pretty amazing.

AND YET YOU'RE HUNG UP?

Maybe on the surface of things there's much to be disgruntled about in your relationship. But stepping back every so often to have a think about how lucky you actually are to be here in the first place should help you start to see your retroactive jealousy a little differently. Believe me, I know how easy it is to always feel put upon and like life's somehow working against you. But it's not. It's just your perception that's making it seem like it is. In reality, your life is amazing and you have someone to share it with. Unlike many, many people. Remind yourself of this whenever your mind seems to determined to drag you down into negativity about the past or future, and take a moment to marvel at just how lucky you are.

There's a scene near the end of the film, *High Fidelity*, in which disgruntled record store owner, Rob (John Cusack), comes home to find his girlfriend, Laura, reading his list of top five dream jobs:

Rob: Hi, Laura.

Laura: (reading) "Top five dream jobs…"

Rob: Hey, that's private.

Laura: "Number one: journalist for *Rolling Stone* magazine, 1976 to 1979. Get to meet *The Clash*, Chrissie Hynde, *The Sex Pistols*, David Byrne. Get tons of free records. Number two: producer for *Atlantic Records*, 1964 to 1971. Get to meet Aretha, Wilson Pickett, Solomon Burke. More free records and a shit load of money. Number three: Any kind of musician — "

Rob: — besides classical or rap.

Laura: "I'd settle for being one of the *Memphis Horns* or something. I'm not asking to be Jagger, or Hendrix, or Otis Redding."

Rob: Uh-huh.

Laura: "Number four: film director."

Rob: Any except German or silent.

Laura: And number five... you have architect...

Rob: Yeah.

Laura: Seven years training...

Rob: I'm not sure I even wanna be an architect.

Laura: So you've got a list here of five things you'd do if qualifications, and time and history and salary were no object?

Rob: Yeah...

Laura: One of them you don't really wanna do anyway?

Rob: Well I did put it at number five.

Laura: Wouldn't you rather own your own record store than be an architect?

Rob: Yeah, I suppose.

Laura: And you wouldn't want to be a sixteenth century explorer, or the king of France...

Rob: God, no.

Laura: (writes) There you go then, dream job number five: record store owner.

Have a go at reframing your perception of what you already have. Maybe you're already living your dream and don't even realize it.

HOW MANY DAYS DO YOU HAVE LEFT?

In the winter of 2013, Wilko Johnson, guitarist with British dad rock band, *Dr Feelgood*, was diagnosed with terminal cancer. He was given under a year left to live. Luckily for him it turned out the doctors were wrong and his condition wasn't terminal, but treatable. "I suddenly felt intensely alive," he remembers. "Everything around me looked sharp and vibrant. I felt free. Free from the future and the past, free from everything but this present moment I was in." In other words, he finally truly valued the time he had on Earth.

I know I've mentioned before that in essence, time is an illusion—there is no past or future, only the now—but the truth is you only have a finite amount of days left to enjoy being alive. Although comparing life expectancies across countries can be problematic, the average lifespan for men in the developed world is around seventy-six to eighty years old. That leaves you with how many years? Exactly. In fifty years time you very well might no longer be here. In a hundred years time you definitely won't be here. Depressing as that may be, it's also an opportunity to open up to life in the now— in this present moment—and to stop taking time (and your life with your partner) for granted.

Let's imagine for a moment that you're thirty. Let's then imagine you live until you're eighty-five. That means you have fifty-five years left. If there are 365 days in a year, that means you have 20,021 days left. And if there are twenty-four hours in a day, that means you have 480,504 hours left. Which means that every hour that goes by is another one out of 480,504 that's lost forever, never to be recaptured. While this can be quite a depressing thought—a thought you maybe spend most of the time trying to avoid—it can also be quite a liberating one. Don't make the mistake of waiting until you're diagnosed with terminal cancer to come out the other side vowing never to take another day of their life for granted. Start now. Start viewing time as a precious commodity and something that you'll never get back.

Forget the old adage of living every day "as if it's your last" because that's just impractical. What's not so impractical, though, is living each day while being more mindful of the present moment and how you use it. It's time to take back your time and stop doing things you don't really want to do just to please other people. Stop watching movies or reading books just because you've started them. Stop spending hours watching drivel on TV. Stop taking your time left on this Earth for granted, because your life—this very moment—is slipping through your fingers. Now, you can either be terrified by this truth, or you can do something about it.

Here's another simple exercise you can start doing every day. Simply say to yourself as often as possible: *I'm enjoying myself*. No matter what you're doing, where you are, or how good or bad your day's actually going, just tell yourself that you're having a blast and watch how it immediately makes the world seem a better place. Try it the next time you're trying to flag down a cab in the rain, or stuck in an elevator with an obnoxious bore, or stuck thinking about your partner's past. You may be surprised.

WRAPPING UP

MOVING FORWARD

Firstly, I want to say that I really appreciate you purchasing this book. Hopefully you feel better having just read it this first time. You've had to take a lot of information while reading it and, as you've probably noticed, relationship jealousy can be a difficult beast to pin down. Its two key emotions are fear and judgment, but there can be a whole host of other contributing factors, such as leading an "unfulfilled" and unchallenging lifestyle, how stressful your life is generally, your personality, diet, genetics, upbringing, and past relationships.

Not only that but I've also thrown a lot of different theories at you regarding the ego, confidence, memory, promiscuity and so on. Some may resonate with you more than others, but that's okay. See which steps make the most sense to you and focus on them. It may take a day. It may take a week. It may take a month, but by doing these exercises these patterns of behavior *will* disappear. The condition of relationship jealousy is not as strong as you think. It's not as strong as you, or your relationship with your partner, and I'm confident that you'll defeat it.

I'd love to hear any feedback you may have on the book, so feel free to contact me. And don't forget to check out my further resources online at:

www.retroactivejealousycrusher.com/resourcestoolkit/

Onward!

Jeff

ABOUT THE AUTHOR

Jeff Billings was born in London, England and has been trying to escape to LA ever since. He is currently living in Brighton on the south coast with his now wife, Emma, plotting this escape. Don't worry, they intend to go together. In the meantime, he is spending his spare time learning jazz piano, reading fifty books a year and avoiding street protests.